this is
Sketched

men

R GINRO

HENRI CARTIER-BRESSON

Photography is an immediate reaction, drawing is a meditation.

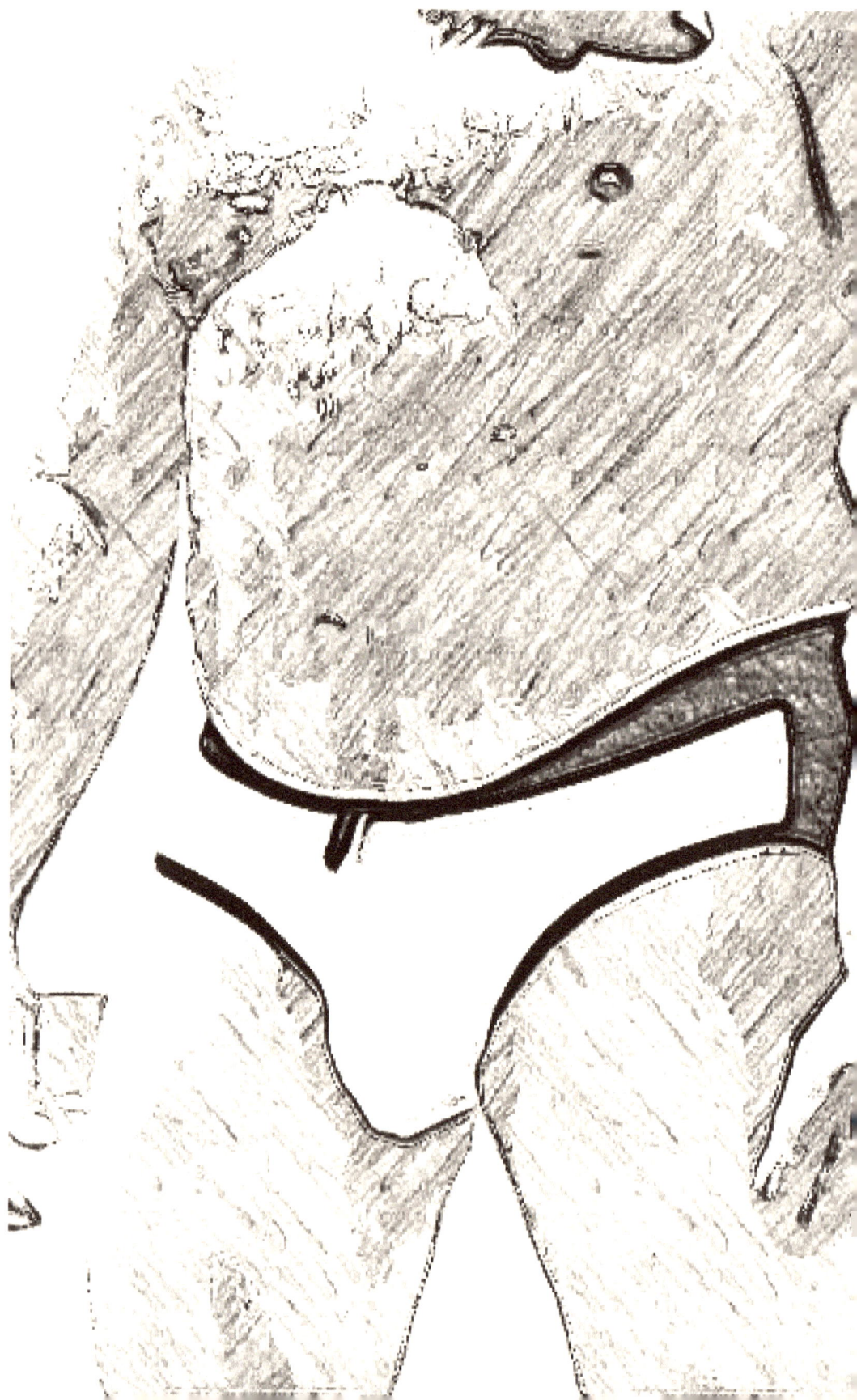

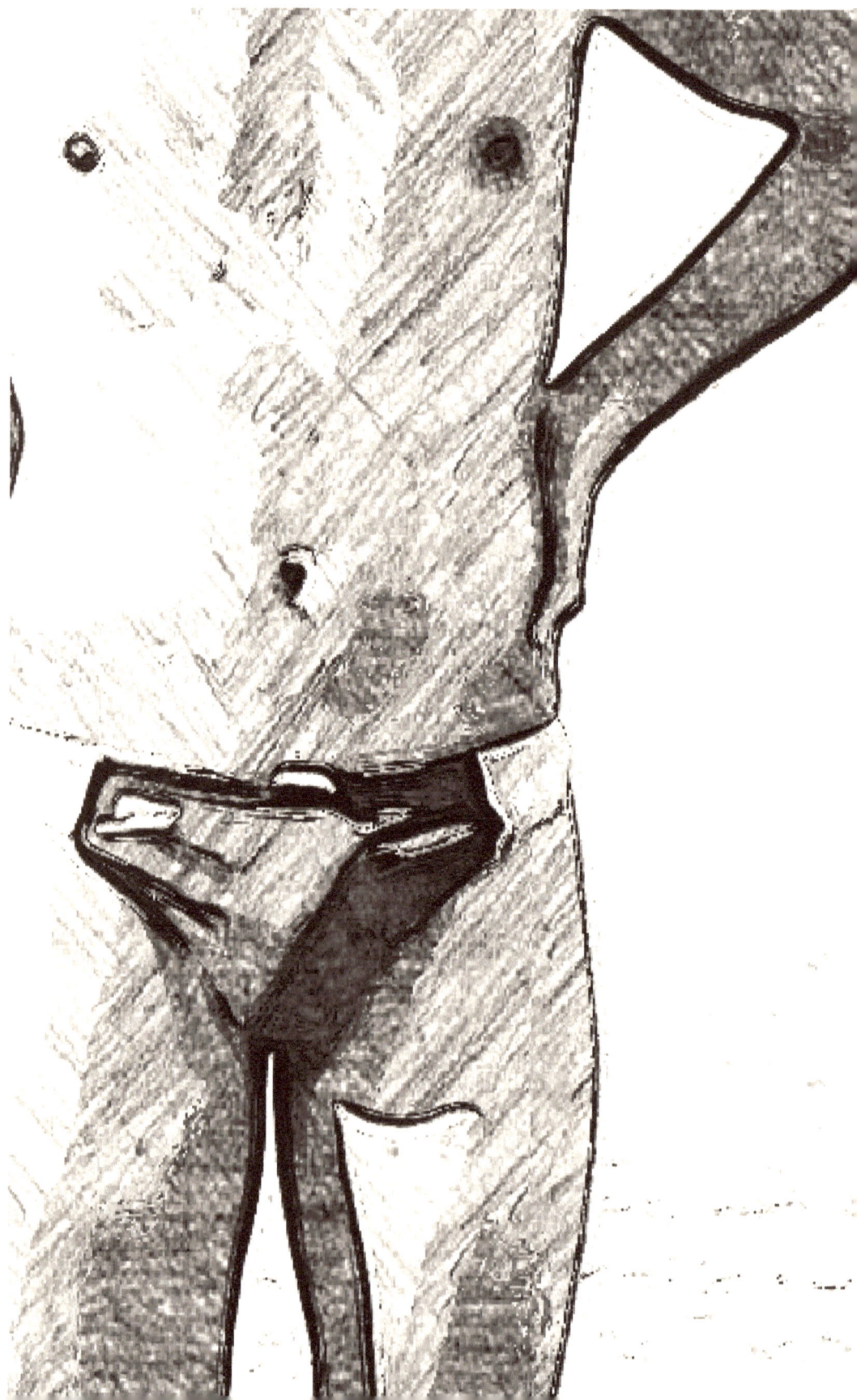

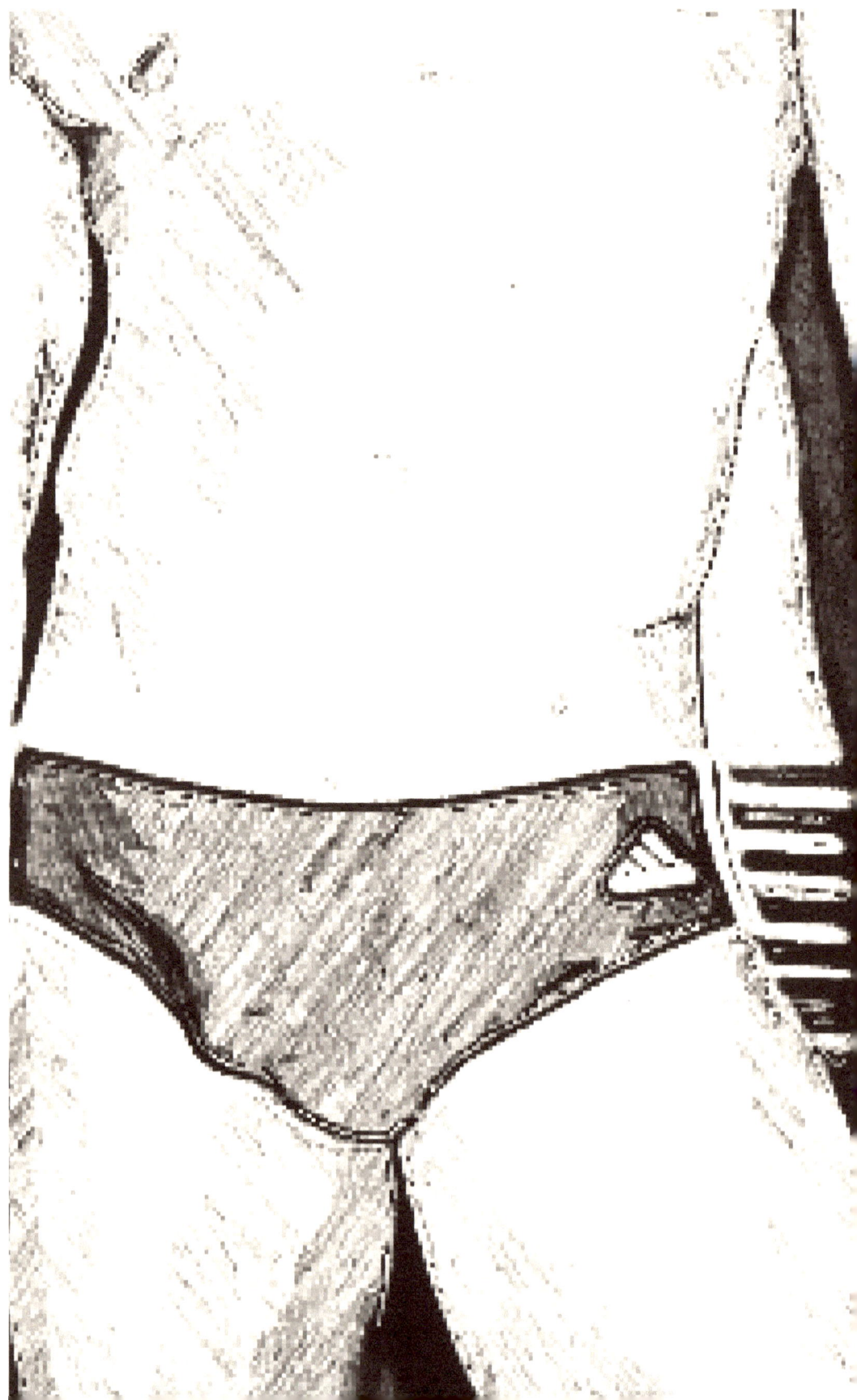

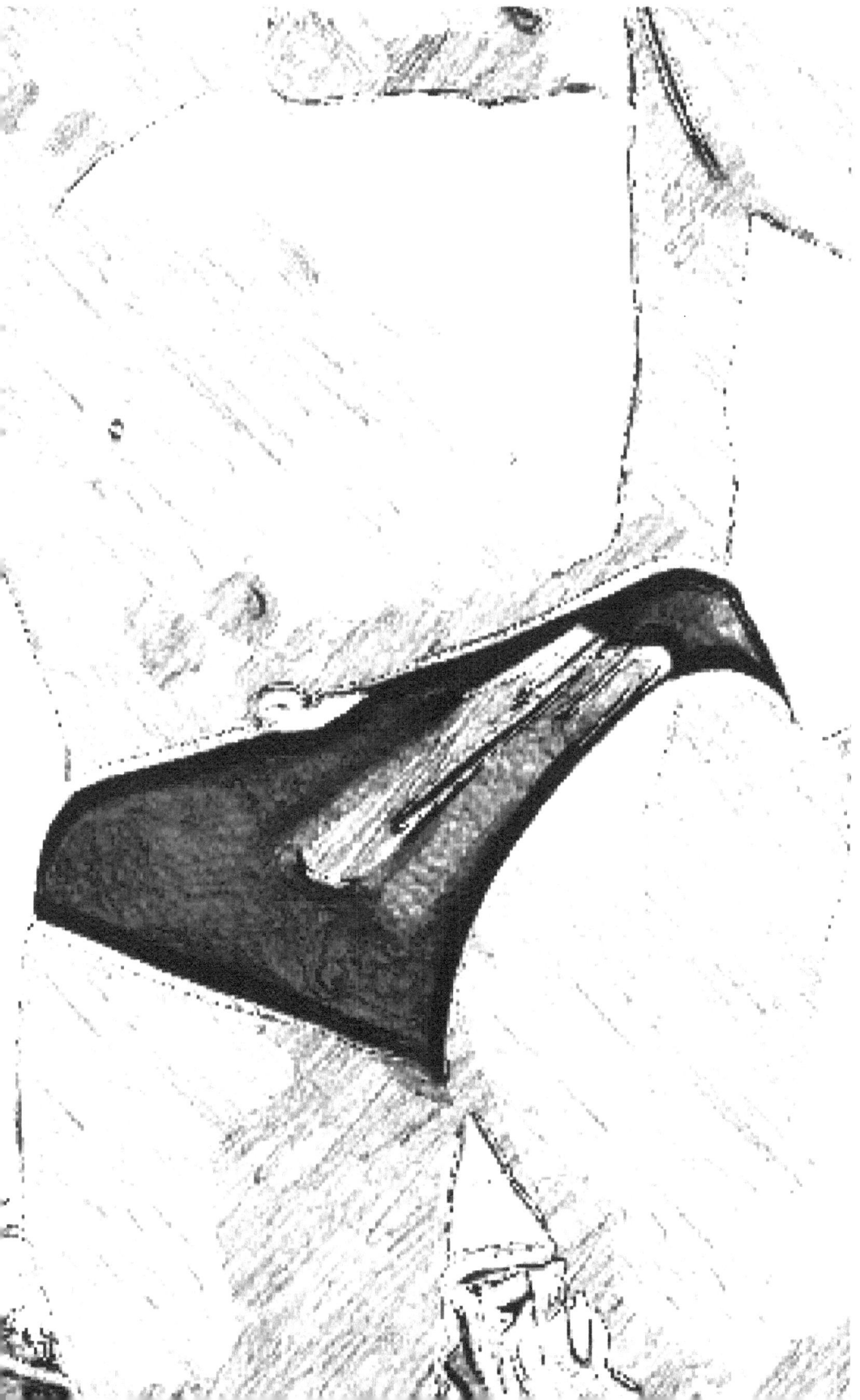

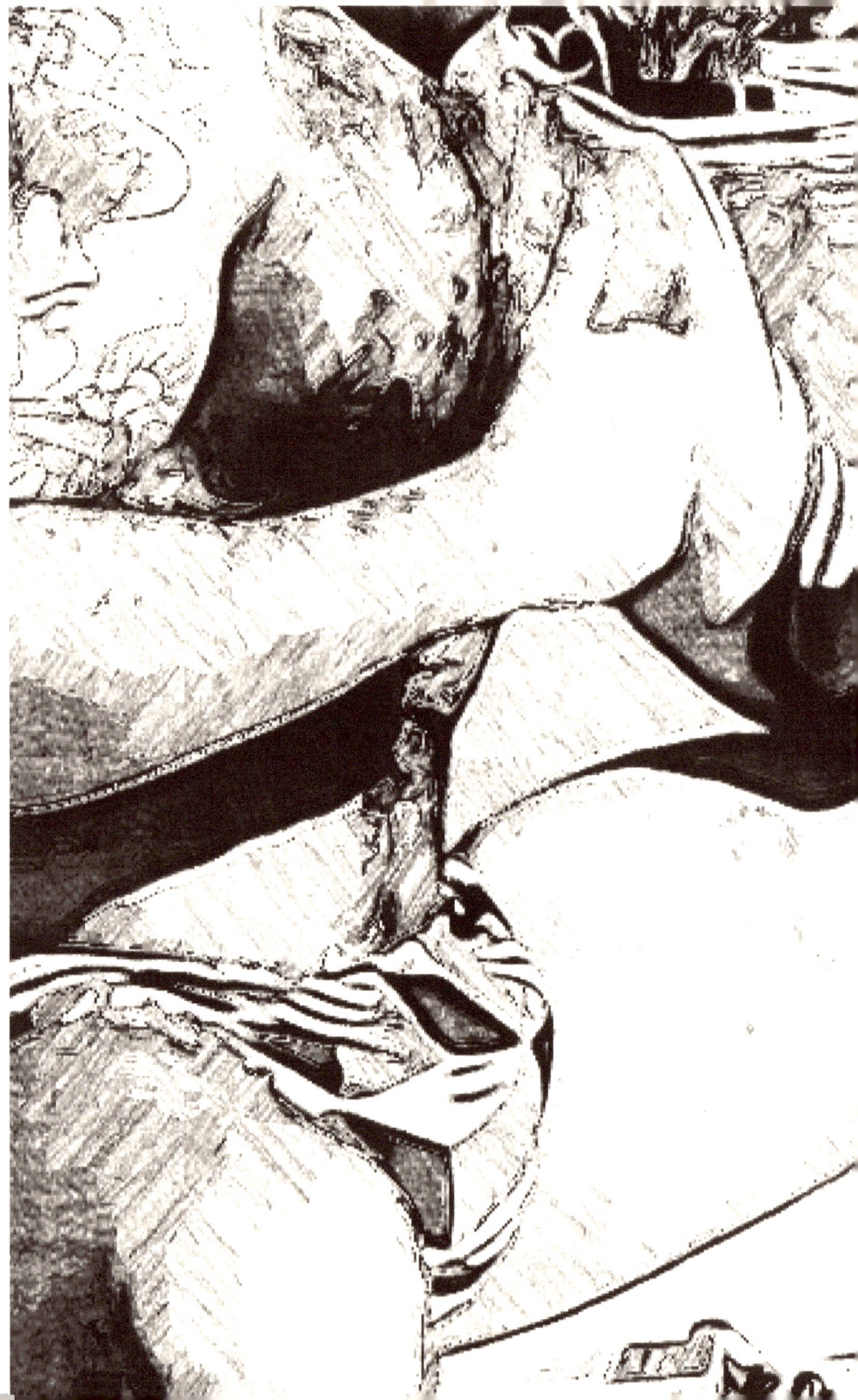

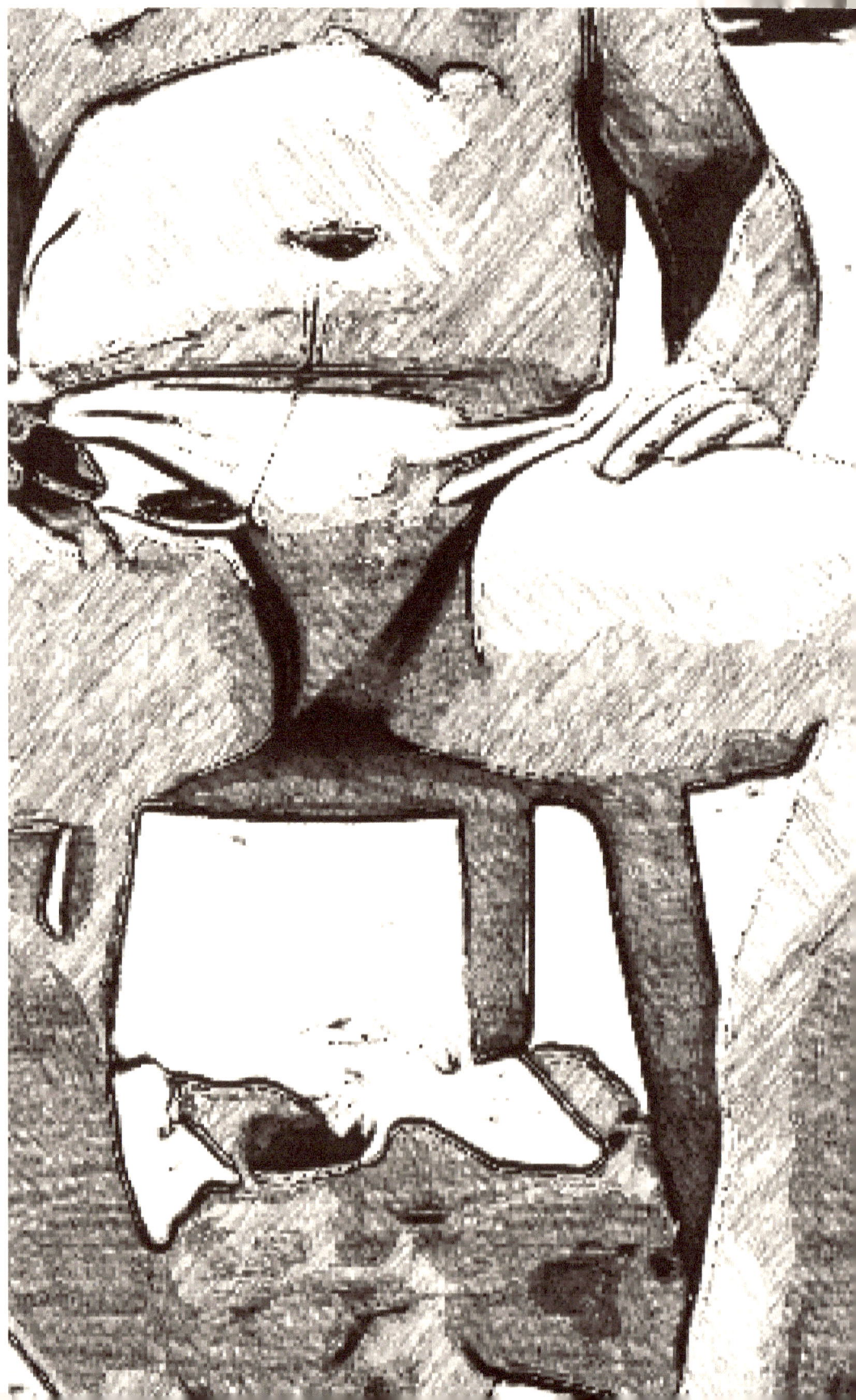

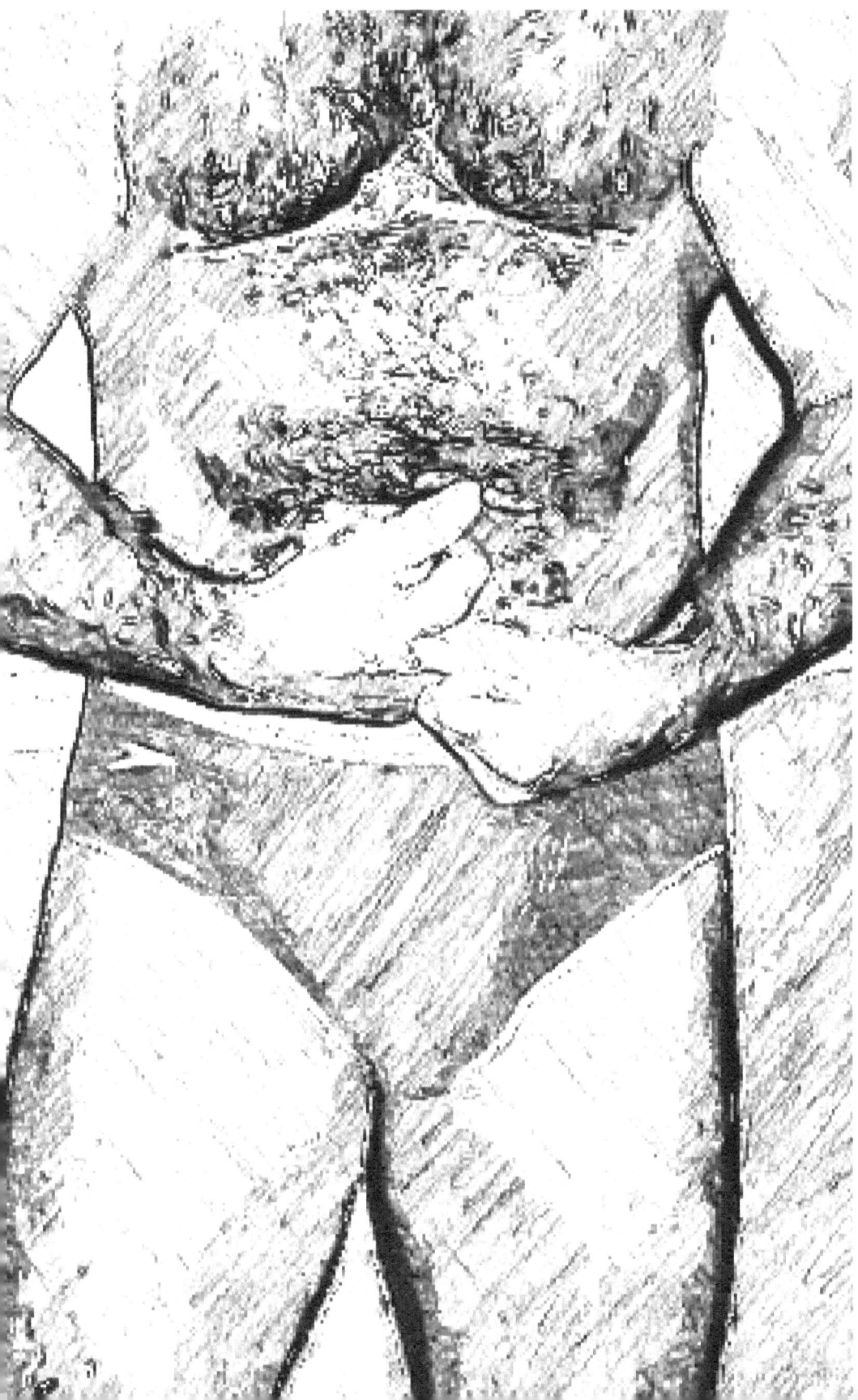

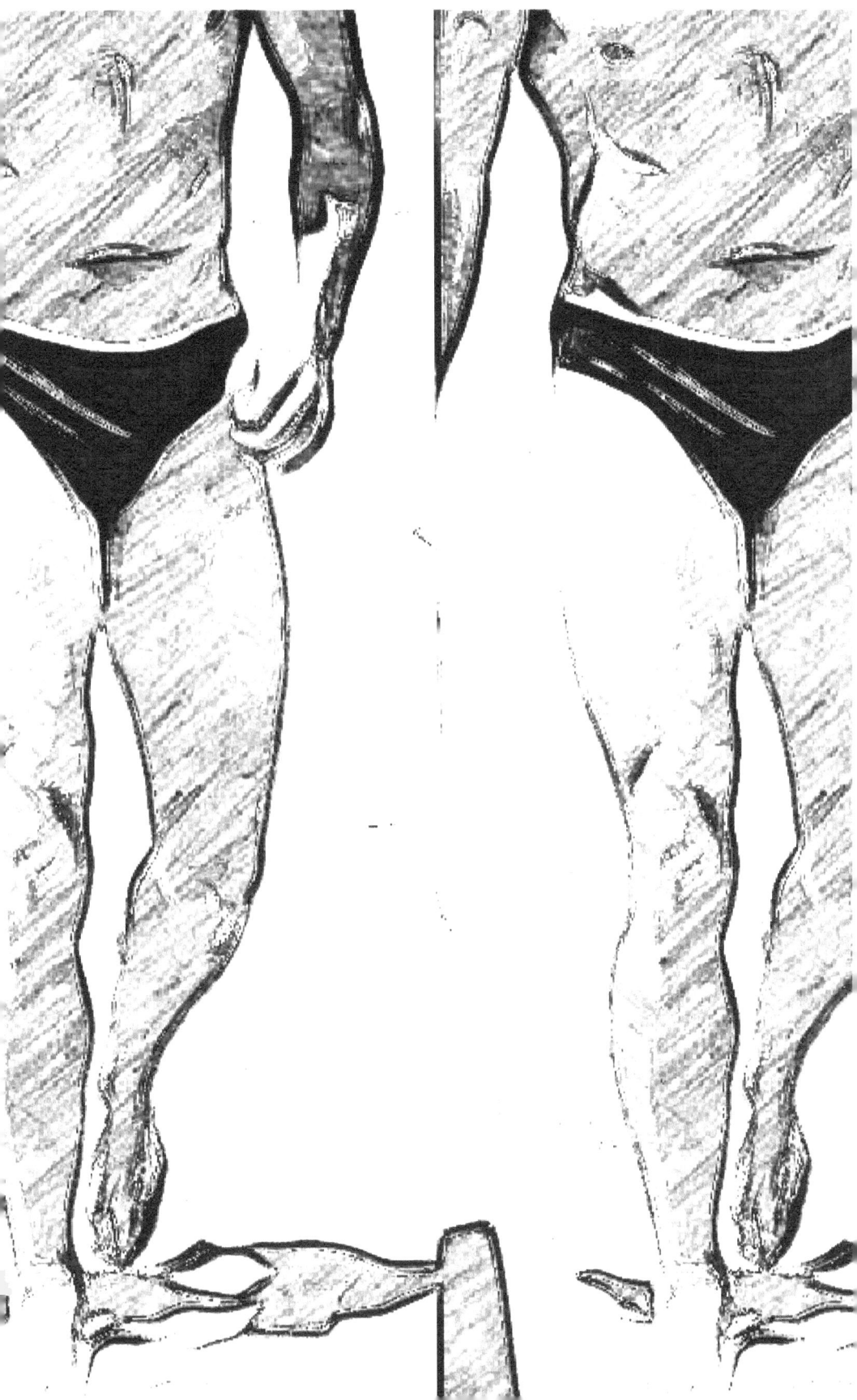

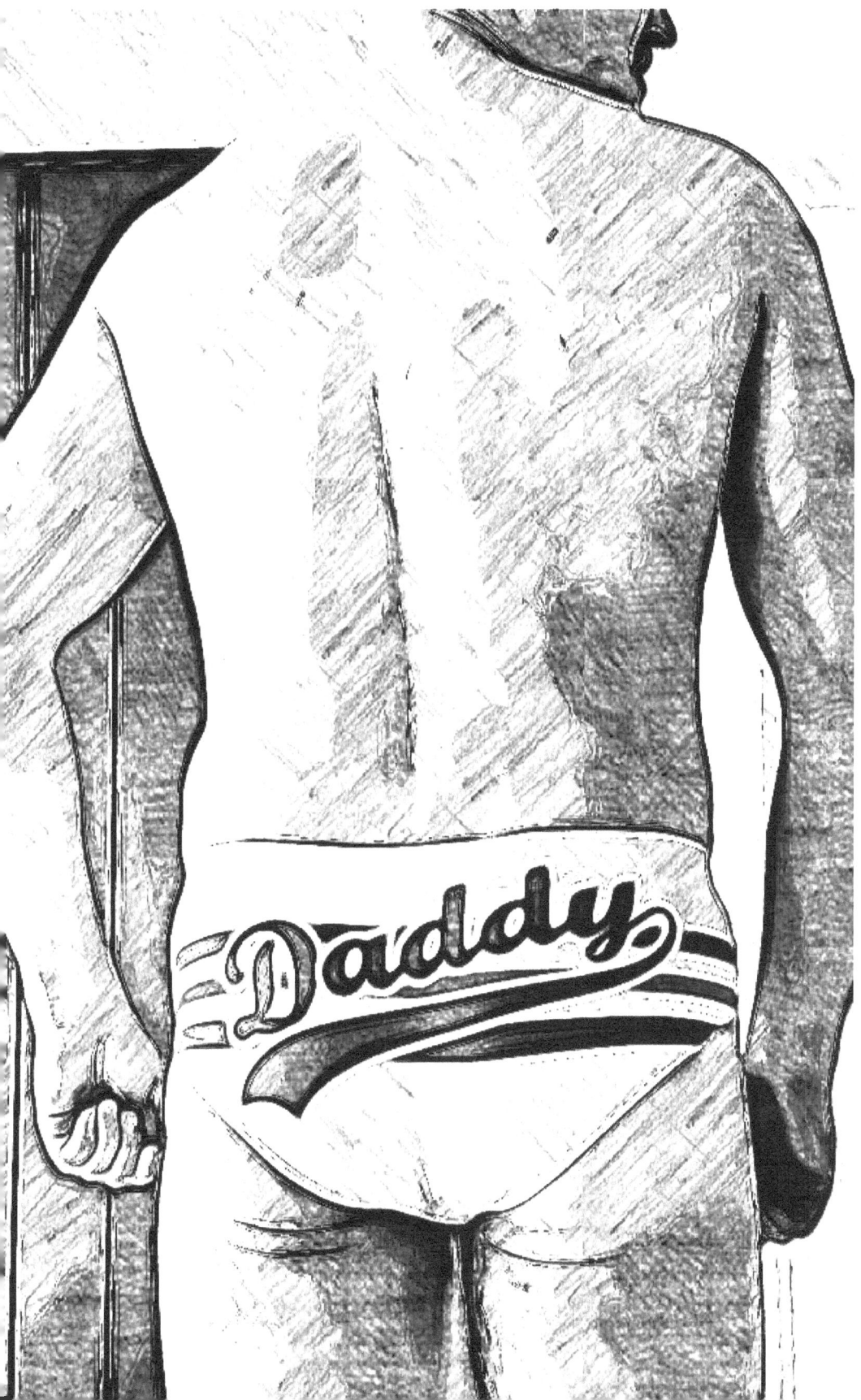

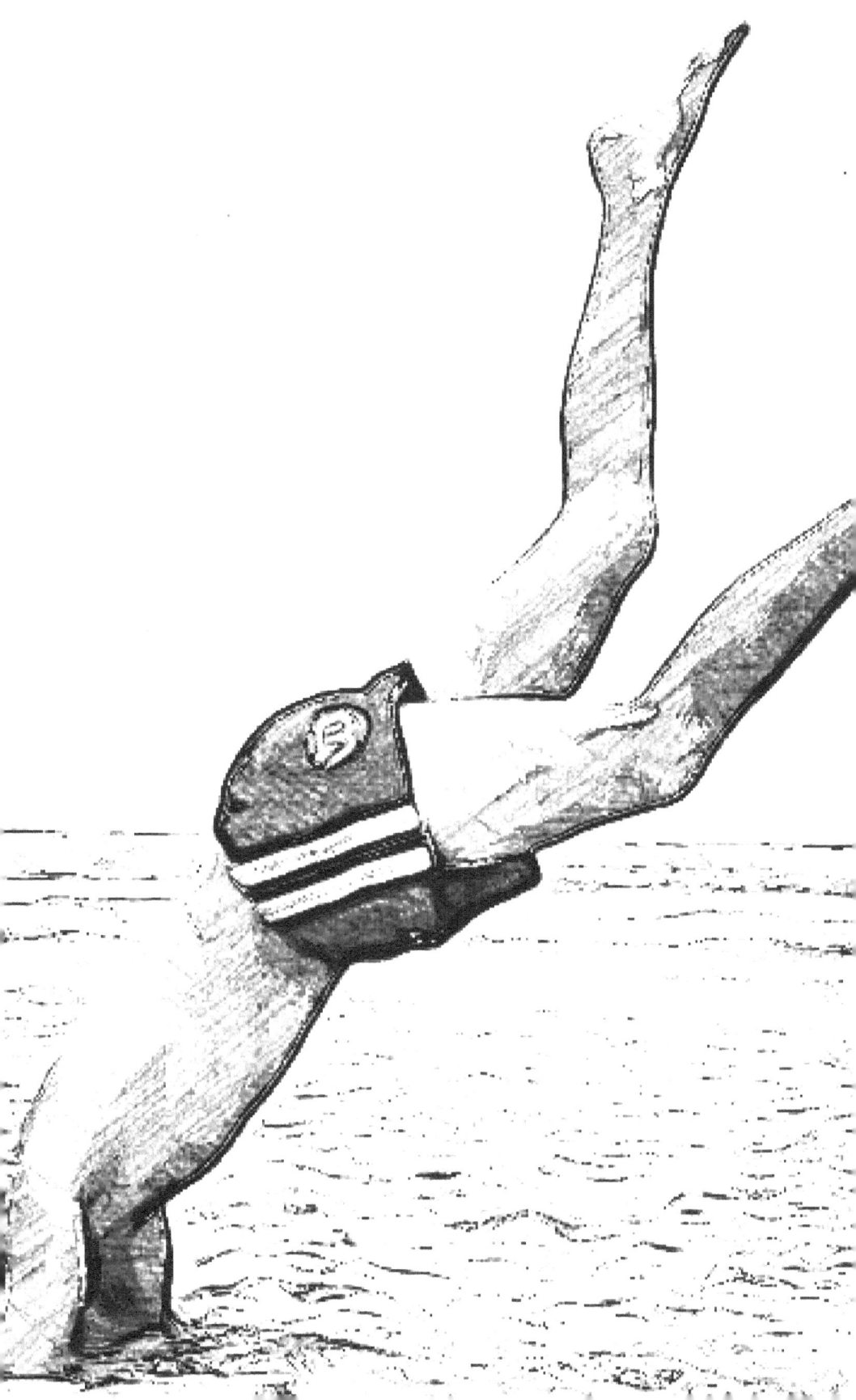

www.ingramcontent.com/pod-product-compliance
Lightning Source LLC
Chambersburg PA
CBHW030908180526
45163CB00004B/1755